Playful Plays (V

This lively collection of short plays for children and young people is supported by inspirational drama games designed to bring creativity and fun to the rehearsal room. The stories are based on traditional folk-tales from countries including China, Ghana, Greece, Japan, Turkey and Scandinavia.

The plays can easily be performed by groups of children and young people on their own, or under the direction of an adult. They feature performance techniques such as mime, mask, freeze frames, audience participation, live music and song.

The author draws on his experience in the professional theatre world to provide helpful advice for the young director and actor including warm-ups, tips on line-learning and ideas for character development, as well as games to develop acting skills such as concentration, focus and working as an ensemble.

David Farmer is a freelance drama consultant, theatre director and author of several best-selling books on drama. His plays have been performed at theatres across London and the UK as well as in schools and festivals across the world.

Also by David Farmer:

101 Drama Games and Activities
101 More Drama Games and Activities
Learning Through Drama in the Primary Years

Playful Plays

Volume 1

David Farmer

Illustrations by Robert Dyer

www.dramaresource.com

Published by Drama Resource

www.dramaresource.com

ISBN: 978-1500630614

Dedicated to all young actors and directors:

Break a leg!

Contents

Introduction

This book is designed to encourage a playful approach to rehearsing and performing plays. The first part outlines a range of warm ups and activities that will help children and young people to explore drama skills and performance techniques. Of course, you may prefer to jump straight to the plays in the second part of the book if you are eager to get started.

The warm-ups are designed to prepare and "tune-up" the actor's body, voice and mind. They can be practised in the order that you find them, or you may pick and choose whatever you need. The activities and drama games introduce simple techniques which can be used in performance. The games are designed to be fun and to encourage a creative and productive atmosphere during rehearsals.

Some plays are adapted from scripts previously performed by a professional theatre in education company, while others were written especially for this book. Every production of a play will be new, fresh and different depending on the actors, director, designers, musicians, prop and costume makers and everyone else involved. So make sure that you make your production one that the audience will not forget in a hurry!

Visit dramaresource.com/playfulplays to receive free resources including:

★   Music files to download and suggestions for other tracks to play

★   Artist illustrations to hang up or colour in

★   Even more drama games, tips and techniques!

Warming Up

Just as musicians must tune their instruments, actors need to warm up their bodies and voices before a rehearsal or performance. The following exercises will raise your heart rate and ensure that your muscles are warm and supple. You will feel more awake in body and mind so that you can put your energy and concentration into your acting. If you want a full warm-up, do all the exercises in order. If you have less time, simply pick the ones that you think you need the most.

Shake out

Stand with your feet slightly apart and shake your hands lightly. Continue by shaking both arms and hands together. Now, stop shaking your arms, lift one foot from the ground and wiggle it. Continue by shaking your whole leg. Swap over to the other leg. Shake your arms again and then your whole body, moving around on the spot. If you like, you can also gently hum while you are doing this – it makes a great sound and is good preparation for warming up the voice.

Relax your shoulders

Roll your shoulders forwards three times, making big circles. Reverse the direction for another three rolls. Next, lift your shoulders high up towards your ears and breathe in deeply. Drop your shoulders as you breathe out. It helps if you make a sighing noise: Aa-aaa-ah! Do this three times. And once more for luck.

At this point you might like to play a warm up game such as *Count to 20* or *Clap Across the Circle* (p.14). These will warm up your body, sharpen your focus and encourage everyone to play around with each other - because after all, that's what acting is all about!

Voice Warm Ups

The way that you use your voice on stage is really important. You should be able to speak loudly enough for everybody to hear you (this is called "projecting your voice") and be able to vary the volume and the way that you speak for different characters and emotions. Using your voice on stage is very different to how you use it day to day, so make sure you use voice exercises while you are rehearsing and before a performance. Vocal warm ups are also great fun as you get to make a lot of noise!

Breathing

When you breathe out, the vocal cords in your throat vibrate to make the sound of your voice. Learning to control your breathing will help to improve the control and power of your voice.

Stand with your feet slightly apart and take a deep breath in through your nose. Sigh the breath out, creating the kind of sound you make when you get home and relax after a busy day. Enjoy the sensation of sighing as you let the tension out of your body. Do this a couple more times. Now as you breath in, take the air right down to your abdomen so that you feel your belly swell. Put your hand there so that you can feel it move. The abdomen is where good breathing control comes from.

As you let the deep breath out, allow your sigh to get slightly louder so that it starts to sound like a yawn. If you practice breathing like this a few more times, it will give your voice more power and help you to project it to the back of the audience.

Yawning and Stretching

Stand with your feet slightly apart, take a deep breath and yawn the air out. Stretch your arms upwards and outwards at the same time, just as you do when you wake up or when you feel tired. Enjoy the sense of relaxation and repeat the action so that altogether you yawn three times.

Start your next yawn on a high note and swoop your voice downwards like a siren. Keep going until you make the lowest note you can. It sounds really good if you can end up with your mouth open making a croaking noise like a frog! This helps to make sure you are keeping your throat relaxed.

Now shake out your whole body to make sure you are not holding any tension.

Humming

A really good way of warming up your voice is to hum. Start with everyone breathing in together and then hum on a high note, slowly swooping down and then up, just like you did for the yawning – except that this time you should have your mouth closed. Keep your feet slightly apart and your body relaxed. If you are too tense it will make your voice sound tight. Spend a few minutes humming until your voice sounds smoother. Try quietly humming a tune that everyone knows, like *Frere Jacques*, for example.

When your voice feels warm, the group may enjoy singing a couple of songs like *Rose, Rose*. The words are below and you can easily find the tune on the internet. It can be sung as a round. Of course, any song that you enjoy singing will be fine.

> *Rose, Rose, Rose, Red*
> *Shall I ever see thee wed?*
> *I marry that I shall*
> *When thou art dead.*

Face Stretch

Now let's get ready to speak some words by warming up the mouth, tongue and lips. Do each exercise for twenty or thirty seconds.

★ Imagine you have a big ball of gum in your mouth. Chew it in the middle of your mouth and then on each side.

★ Next, can you relax your lips and blow some air through them? We call this sound 'horse blowing'. Make sure that you are not facing directly at other people as they may get wet!

★ Screw your face up as tight as you can and then open it wide, with an open mouth and wide eyes.

Tongue Twisters

Tongue twisters help you get used to the feel and shape of words. It's fun trying to say them quickly, but also make sure you say each syllable as clearly as you can.

The lips, the teeth, the tip of the tongue,
The tip of the tongue, the teeth, the lips.

Moses supposes his toes-es are roses,
But Moses supposes erroneously[1].

Around the rugged rocks the ragged rascal ran.

A box of biscuits, a box of mixed biscuits and a biscuit mixer.

Which wrist watch is a Swiss wrist watch?

---

1 From the song by Eden, Comden and Green featured in *Singin' in the Rain* (MGM 1952).

Drama Games

Now that you have warmed up your body and voice you can start rehearsing the play. Or, you could play some drama games. As well as being fun, these help everybody to focus on what they're doing, to work together and to feel confident. Some games even help to generate ideas which can be used in performance, as well as developing acting, characterisation and movement skills.

Count To 20

Every one stands in a circle. The aim is for the whole group to count to twenty, with only one person saying one number at a time. Anybody can start, and anyone else can say the next number. But if two or more people speak at the same time, counting has to start again from the beginning. This can seem difficult at first because nobody knows who will say the next number!

The game is all about learning to concentrate and focus as a group. If everybody really listens and pays attention then it is possible to get to twenty. Try asking everybody to take a deep breath and to sigh out before they start. This can help the group to work together.

Of course you may be very lucky and get to twenty straight away, but most groups will need to practice. Don't spend too long on it; if it doesn't work try again another day!

Clap Across The Circle

Here's a game that's quick to learn but which requires everyone to be wide awake and to make eye-contact, a very important skill for actors.

The actors stand in a circle and one person (the clapper) starts by making eye contact with someone else (the receiver) on the other side of the circle. The clapper claps her hands and at the same time moves her hands towards the receiver as though she is throwing the sound across the circle. The receiver claps his hands a short distance away from his body as though catching the sound that the clapper has made and then brings his hands towards his body. This will look almost like an invisible ball has been passed across the circle.

Now we have a new clapper who must clap across the circle to someone else. Don't forget to make eye-contact before you clap, otherwise no-one will know who you are aiming at! Once people get good at this they can try throwing the clap in different ways - up in the air, bouncing it on the ground, quickly, slowly, lightly or heavily.

Trickster

This is an adaptation of *Follow the Leader* with a twist. One person (the 'Trickster') randomly chooses different leaders so that everyone is kept on their toes! The game helps actors become more aware of what everyone else is doing on stage and how to change the focus – two useful skills.

Everyone spreads out around the room, standing in a space on their own. The Trickster chooses the first Leader by tapping someone on the shoulder. The Leader makes simple movements for everybody else to copy, changing them from time to time. While this is happening the Trickster moves around the space and randomly chooses a new Leader by tapping someone else on the shoulder. Everyone (and that includes the previous Leader) should be ready to copy the actions of the new Leader straight away.

The Leader can move around – and of course everyone else should move too. This is both challenging and fun as it becomes harder to see the Leader the whole time and the Trickster may change the Leader at any moment.

Tips

★ Whoever is the Leader should try to come up with new ideas for movements, as well as varying the pace – otherwise everyone will get worn out very quickly!

★ Try using sounds as well as movements.

★ The Trickster should try to catch people out by changing the Leader when they are least expecting it.

Family Portraits

In this game, small groups have just a few seconds to create funny family portraits by striking interesting poses. Everyone gets into groups of about five or six, spread around the space. Explain that you are going to call out the name of a type of family and each group has to create a freeze-frame of that family in just five seconds. They should try to include different age-groups including children, adults and grandparents.

Call out the name of a family from the list opposite and count down from five to zero. Ask everybody to hold the freeze for a few moments so that you can look at all the portraits and then invite one or two groups to show what they've done.

Once the players have got the hang of the game, try out a few more – and make up some families of your own. The tableaux are bound to be amusing, so you can ask groups to share what they came up with.

Tips

Encourage the players to look at what other people in their group are doing so that they make contrasting characters, show different expressions and use varying levels to make an interesting stage picture (it's amazing what you can achieve in just a few seconds).

Develop

After a few rounds, ask the groups to devise their own families for the rest of the class to guess. They should try to show the relationships between characters and may even include pets!

Some of the examples below are related to the plays in this book, while others are just for fun. Simply add the word 'family' after each one.

Angry	Greek Gods	Rats
Astronaut	Jungle Animals	Robbers
Chicken	Market Traders	Royal
Circus	Peculiar	Sleepy
Dancing	Partying	Street Buskers
Geeky	Proud	Theatrical

Ten Second Objects

Everybody gets into groups of about five. Explain that you will call out the name of an object and each group should make the shape of that object out of their own bodies in only ten seconds. Now call out the first object and start counting down from ten to zero. Choose something easy to begin with, such as a car.

Everyone needs to work together very quickly to make sure they are finished within ten seconds. Usually each group will find an interesting and amusing way of forming the object. Ask some or all of the groups to show what they made. You can ask the other groups to make some positive comments. and point out what was most particularly effective (for example using different levels - high, medium and low).

Groups can also be given a minute to discuss and devise an object for the rest of the class to guess. You can set a theme such as household objects (e.g. washing machine, clock, television, sofa) or the city, the countryside, the seaside and so on.

Here is a selection of fun objects to make:

Bunch of bananas	Helicopter	Robot
Clock	Jungle	Shower
Elephant	Palace	Snowflake
Fire	Pirate ship	Spectacles
Flower	Plate of food	Umbrella

The game is good practice for making objects to use in performance. The audience will enjoy seeing the actors making objects – and this approach can be more fun than using real props (and cheaper too).

UPSTAGE RIGHT	UPSTAGE	UPSTAGE LEFT
STAGE RIGHT	CENTRE STAGE	STAGE LEFT
DOWNSTAGE RIGHT	DOWNSTAGE	DOWNSTAGE LEFT

Using the Stage

Left, Right, Centre?

When you direct a play, you will sometimes need to tell the actors where to move to. If you ask them to move to the right, do you mean your right or their right? To solve this problem we talk about left and right from the point of view of the actor (see stage diagram on p.18). We use the terms *Stage Right* and *Stage Left* (or SR and SL).

If we ask the actors to move forwards or backwards, we come across the same problem and for this reason we use the terms *Upstage* and *Downstage* (in a traditional theatre the stage was always higher at the back than at the front to help the audience see all the actors).

If you combine these terms you can say things like "Please hop to Upstage Right" or "Exit dramatically Downstage Left". If you make sure that you and the actors understand these instructions then rehearsals will run a lot more smoothly. You can make it fun to learn these names by playing the game *Upstage/Downstage*[1].

Stage Pictures

An important job for the actors and director is creating the stage picture. This is the overall image showing what's going on in a scene at any particular moment. When the audience looks at the stage they need to know where the focus is (which part of the scene is most important for them to look at). They should be able to see all the characters and their facial expressions so that they can understand what is happening between them.

The next couple of games help the cast to practise creating stage pictures, which can be used to inspire ideas for a scene.

---

1 *101 More Drama Games and Activities* (Farmer 2012) p.42.

19

I Am A...

The actors stand in a big circle and a theme is announced. Whoever thinks of the first idea steps forward and makes a still image of an object or character related to the theme. As well as making the shape, the actor should announce what she is, for example if the theme is the garden of King Midas, the actor can say "I am a garden gnome" or "I am King Midas".

Other players add themselves into the scene by making objects or characters related to ones that are already there (announcing what they are each time). Everyone continues to hold their positions. The game ends when all the players have stepped in or when plenty of ideas have been added. At this point the director says "Whoosh!" and the actors step back to the edge of the circle.

Only one idea at a time should be added to the stage picture so that everyone can see and hear what is being included. The actors should think about how their characters and objects relate to each other, how they can make interesting shapes and how they can use different levels (high, medium or low).

It's best if the actors don't plan too much but just keep throwing in new ideas. Instead of judging which objects and characters are 'best', try using the game as a brainstorming activity to create inspiring ideas for the director and the actors to choose from. It can be helpful to take photos of the finished stage picture for future reference.

Tips

★ Two or more actors can step into the circle at the same time if they think of an object to make together.

★ If the scene looks particularly interesting, the director can say "Action!" and everyone can bring the scene alive for a few moments through improvised sound and action.

You can choose a theme from a play you are working on or try one of these:

Beach, rainforest, outer space, under the sea, kitchen, museum, classroom, hospital, royal palace, city street, gym, TV studio, toy box, Olympic stadium, farmyard...

Make Me A...

This is an even quicker way to make stage pictures. Divide the actors into groups of about five or six. Clap your hands and ask them to "Make me a..." while you count down from five to zero, for example "Make me a spooky forest." The actors should create a tableau (freeze-frame) containing characters and/or objects – *with as little talking as possible.* You can choose a fun theme for a warm-up or any topic related to the play you are rehearsing.

Below are a few suggestions to try out:

A proud family... a street fight... a shipwreck... a spooky forest... a battlefield... a busy market-place... King Midas turning his son into gold... a lively party... a group of robbers planning their next job... witches casting a spell...

The more the actors play these games, the faster they will come up with interesting ideas for staging a scene, which will make the director's job that much easier. As they become more practised, ask them to think about *sight lines*[2], so that they make sure it is possible for the audience to see everything that is going on in the scene.

---

2 See Glossary (p.124-5).

Whoosh!

Once the actors have practised making stage pictures with the previous two games, they will be ready to act out a story. Whoosh! is an exciting way of creating a live performance through instant storytelling, giving everyone a chance to take part as characters, objects and even locations. It is suitable for any age-group as it can be used with virtually any story.

The storyteller asks the actors to sit or stand in a circle. Explain that the participants will act out the story you tell by stepping into the space to make an object or character. Sometimes they will have actions to do or words to speak. When you say "Whoosh!" and wave your arms, everyone should return to their places around the circle.

Start telling the story and as soon as you mention a character, event or object, point to the first player to step into the circle. If two or more characters are introduced they can step in together. You can even pick several actors to step in at once – for example as a forest. If there are sound effects, then the people sitting in the circle can make them.

Keep telling the story with the players in the centre acting it out. When you mention new characters or objects just pick the next person along to take part. You may need to pause as actors step into the circle to take up their places. Continue telling the story and building up the scene. Characters can interact with and speak to each other by repeating lines read out by the storyteller or by making up their own words.

Any time you think that it is too busy or crowded inside the circle, or you have got to the end of a scene, wave your arms and say "Whoosh!" All the actors should return to their places. Continue to tell the story with players stepping in as required. Go around the circle in order so that participants get the chance to play different characters.

Choose a story that has plenty of characters or objects such as fairy tales, traditional stories or Shakespeare plots. Whoosh! can be used to tell the whole or just part of a story. You can tell it from memory or read it from a book (although it is helpful if you can watch what is going on).

You don't need props or costumes as people pretending to be objects is limitless and very entertaining. However you could experiment by adding a few props to play with. This is a fantastic way of creating ideas for a play.

 Tip:

The Midas Touch on page 53 is designed to be used with Whoosh! so why not give it a try?

Creating Characters

The audience are usually very interested in what the characters get up to in a play. What the characters say and do in each scene shows how they feel and what sort of people they are. Actors can develop a character in many ways, but the first place to start is by looking at the script. Sometimes it's easy to understand why characters do what they do but at other times an actor will need to guess why a character behaves in a particular way. Every actor will play a character differently, depending on their own personality and the decisions they make when they are rehearsing. The director can help the actor by making suggestions during rehearsals and by using some of the games and techniques below.

Follow Your Nose

This game shows how the way a character moves says a lot about them. By moving around in different ways, the actors will discover many characters.

The players begin by walking around the room, filling up the space, changing pace and direction. Next, the leader calls out a part of the body, such as the nose. Everybody becomes aware of their own nose and lets it lead them through the space. After a while, stop the actors and pick one or two people to show how they were moving. Ask for suggestions from those watching about characters who might move like this. Perhaps someone very inquisitive – or "nosey"!

Once you have done this, everyone starts moving again and the leader calls out a different body part. Try following your tummy, chin, big toe, left knee, chest, little finger, right ear, shoulder, arm and hips. Each time, ask a few players to show what they were doing. It is likely that you will see lots of different character types. When you return to rehearsal, the actors will be equipped with plenty of ideas to try out.

Hot seating

Hot seating is a fun way of exploring the background and personality of characters. An actor playing a character is questioned by the rest of the group and makes up answers on the spur of the moment. This often brings unusual insights into the character.

One person sits on a chair in front of the group. Members of the audience start asking questions which may include facts like name, age and occupation as well as more personal issues such as likes and dislikes or reasons for behaving in particular ways. Some answers given by the actor may be based on known facts but it is likely that many responses will have to be made up. These are often the most interesting and amusing.

Hot seating gives the actor a chance to enjoy being in role and allows the audience to find out why a character behaved as they did. It doesn't matter if the actor doesn't know every fact about the character – it's not supposed to be a test of knowledge. If you encourage questions about personal feelings and motivations you may be surprised by how much detail can be invented at the drop of a hat!

Tips

★ Audiences can get over-enthusiastic with asking questions or trying to find out tricky facts so you will need one (bossy) person to be in charge of picking questions and guiding the discussion.

★ You can add a touch of fun by playing the role of a chat show host who introduces the character to the audience and guides the questions.

★ If the actors are very young, new to hot seating or particularly nervous then they can be interviewed in twos or threes. This will usually boost their confidence.

Sound Effects and Music

Well-chosen sound effects can help to make plays exciting and realistic. They allow you to instantly create the atmosphere of a jungle, a market square or a storm at sea. Sound effects also create opportunities for other people to get involved if they are not acting in the show. Some effects can be made 'live' while the play is being performed using musical instruments or other objects.

Live Sound Effects

You can buy special thunder shakers and ocean drums, but home-made instruments work just as well. **Thunder** can be made by shaking a thin sheet of aluminium and **rain** can be created by dropping rice onto a drum or sheet of metal. The sound of the **sea** can be made by rolling dried peas around on a large tray or tambour. And don't forget good old coconut shells for **horse** or **donkey hooves** – they really are quite convincing!

Recorded Sound Effects

You may decide to record all the sounds before you do the show. You can use a tape-recorder, computer, digital recorder or smart phone. The effects can be made using objects and musical instruments or you can record actual sounds, such as a creaking door or footsteps. If you really can't make it yourself, you can probably download an MP3 file or buy a sound effects CD.

However you make your effects, it's important to practice playing them back while the actors are rehearsing so that they get used to them. This will also help you find the right volume so that the effects can be heard without drowning out the actors' voices. Try to use the best sound system you can so that the effects sound realistic. Most school halls already have a sound system you can plug into.

Music

Recorded or live music helps to establish or change the mood of a scene. Choose fast music for an exciting scene or slow music for a sad moment. Often you don't need to play the music for very long – just enough for the audience to get the feel of it and then you can fade it out. For some scenes you may want to play the music while the action is happening, such as the tug of war (p.39-40), the journey of the rats (p.47-8), the scene in Nasreddin's house (p. 79-81) or the party scene (p.81). The right music can inspire the actors as well as the audience.

Voices

The most versatile instrument of all is the human voice. Don't forget that it can be fun to create inspiring and atmospheric backgrounds using vocal sound effects. The sound of the wind and other weather can easily be created, as well as animal calls, traffic, crowds, creaking doors and much more. If a group of you are making the sounds it helps to have one person acting as a conductor so that people know when to begin and end and when to raise or lower the volume.

Learning Lines

The best way to learn lines is to keep practising them. You can do this on your own or with friends and family. Here are ten different ways to help those lines stick.

1. Read the lines aloud. By speaking the lines you will hear them and they are more likely to remain in your memory.

2. Ask a friend to help you. Friends can correct you on any mistakes you make, give you the cue lines and go back over any weak areas.

3. Practise little and often. Go over your lines first thing in the morning, a few times during the day and last thing at night.

4. Make a recording of the scene with an audio recorder or smart phone. Read all the other characters' lines but leave a gap when it's your turn to speak. Play it back and say your lines when there is a gap.

5. Make a recording of the whole cast reading the script and use this to practise with so that you get used to hearing the other characters' voices. Or just ask some of your friends to read the parts of different characters.

6. Move around while you are saying your lines. This has been scientifically proven to aid memory. The best thing to do is to act and feel the emotions of the character so that you are learning the meaning of the speech – not just the words. Or just for a change you could do something entirely unrelated like juggling, kicking a ball or dancing around.

7. Go for a walk. Walking and saying your lines can be quite relaxing (though beware of strange looks from passers-by).

8. Learn the cue lines that lead in to each of your lines. Being ready with your lines will give you and your fellow actors more confidence.

9. As you say or read the lines, follow the thought pattern of each speech and the story of each scene. Remember that your lines are a part of the play. They don't exist on their own.

10. In rehearsals, really listen to and think about what the other actors are saying. Don't just concentrate on what you've got to say. This will also make your character seem more realistic. After all we usually listen to each other in real life, don't we?

The Plays

The Tug Of War

Based on a traditional story found in southern and East Africa.

Estimated running time: 6 minutes.

CAST: 4 (M/F)

Hare, *a Trickster*

Hare's Wife

Hippo, *Hare's Aunt*

Elephant, *Hare's Uncle*

Director's Notes

This short play is ideal for a small group. There is plenty of action and not too many lines to learn, so it shouldn't take long to rehearse.

You will need: A rope long enough to go across the stage. Simple costumes such as a shower cap and scrubbing brush for Hippo. Music for the tug of war and sound effects[1].

 Tip:

Playing Animal Characters

The animal characters in these plays should be more human than beast. Think about the behaviour of the animals and the personality of the characters. Choose a couple of the animal's traits, such as a gruff voice for a dog, a hopping step for a hare or a twitchy nose for a rat. Read through the script until you have a clear idea of the character's personality.

Instead of using animal masks, try focussing on facial expression, voice and movement. Play *Follow your Nose* (p.24) to help you explore different ways of moving. Then choose a simple costume piece such as a hat, scarf, pair of glasses or jacket to help you express the character.

---

1 See www.dramaresource.com/playfulplays for suggested music tracks.

HARE is asleep. He wakes up, stretches and yawns.

HARE: What a lovely sunny day! Time to eat a juicy carrot from my garden.

HARE searches around his garden.

HARE: What, no carrots? *(Looking at the audience.)* All I can see are weeds. Disgusting. *(Calls out.)* Wife, where are the carrots?

HARE'S WIFE enters.

HARE'S WIFE: There are no carrots left. You've eaten them all!

HARE: But I'm hungry!

HARE'S WIFE: Well then, you need to plant some more. You can start by digging up all those weeds!

HARE'S WIFE exits.

HARE: Dig up all the weeds? It's far too hot for that. *(Thinks.)* I've got a much better idea.

HARE looks around and finds a long coil of rope. He puts it over his shoulder and walks off.

HIPPO enters, wearing a bath cap and holding a sponge or scrubbing brush.

HIPPO: Here it is. The water hole. Wet and muddy as usual. Nice!

HIPPO holds her nose and jumps in the water hole.

SOUND EFFECT: Water splash (cymbal crash).

HIPPO happily starts to scrub herself, humming a tune. HARE sneaks in.

HARE: Boo!

HIPPO: Oh, Hare, you gave me quite a fright.

HARE: Sorry, Aunty Hippo. Would you play a game with me, please?

HIPPO: Can't you see that I'm busy right now? I'm having a bath!

HARE: I wondered if you would have a tug of war with me? I've got the rope here.

HIPPO: A tug of war? Don't be so silly. I'll soon beat you. Everyone knows a hippo is much stronger than a hare.

HARE: I've been working out lately and I feel quite strong.

HIPPO: Well, if you really insist. But don't say I didn't warn you!

HARE: Thanks, Aunty Hippo. Hold on to this end of the rope. I'll go and stand in the jungle over there. When you feel me tug on the rope, start pulling.

HIPPO: *(Laughing)* Don't worry, I'll be ready, Hare.

HIPPO ties the rope around her waist. She carries on scrubbing and enjoying herself.
HARE walks across the stage.

SOUND EFFECT: ELEPHANT'S feet (loud drum).

HARE: *(To audience.)* I wonder who that could be coming through the jungle?

ELEPHANT enters and meets HARE on the opposite side of the stage to HIPPO.

ELEPHANT: *(Suspiciously)* Hello Hare, what are you up to?

HARE: Nothing much, Uncle.

ELEPHANT: Well, get out of my way, then. I'm going to the water hole for a wash and a drink.

HARE: Just before you go, Uncle, would you play tug of war with me? I've been working out you see, and I want to show you how strong I am.

ELEPHANT: Don't be daft, Hare, you'll never beat me. I'm the strongest animal in the jungle!

HARE: You don't know until you try. If you win, I'll do anything for you. I'll even scrub your back at the water hole.

ELEPHANT looks dubious.

HARE: I'll be your servant for the whole day.

ELEPHANT: Well…

HARE: Here, I'll just tie this rope around your waist. Then I'll go towards the water hole. When you feel me give a little tug on the rope, start pulling.

ELEPHANT: If you say so, Hare.

HARE ties the rope around ELEPHANT. HARE walks to Centre Stage and gives a tug on the rope in each direction. He hides and watches what happens.

MUSIC: Live drumming or recorded African music. HIPPO and ELEPHANT start pulling. First one starts to win, then the other. As they move they shuffle their feet on the floor. They should act as though they can't see each other.

ELEPHANT: *(Grunting)* Perhaps my nephew has been working out.

HIPPO: *(Puffing)* I didn't know Hare was so strong!

ELEPHANT: He must be an Olympic champion!

HIPPO: He's pulling me out of my bath!

                Eventually HIPPO and ELEPHANT start to pull the rope in, so that they get closer and closer to each other.

                MUSIC ends. HIPPO and ELEPHANT see each other.

HIPPO: Elephant?

ELEPHANT: Hippo! What are you doing here?

HIPPO: I don't believe it. Where's Hare? That rascal causes nothing but trouble. Next time I see him, he'll be for it!

ELEPHANT: When I catch him, I'll make him scrub my back, polish my tusks and do all my laundry.

                HIPPO and ELEPHANT exit. HARE comes out of his hiding place, rubbing his hands together.

HARE: Well, there's nothing like a good tug of war to plough the fields! Look at the mud, all churned up. The weeds are gone! My garden is just ready to plant the carrots.

HARE'S WIFE enters.

HARE'S WIFE: Well, well Hare. All the weeds are gone. I didn't believe you had it in you. You are a hard worker after all. Let me make you a nice cup of dandelion tea while you put your feet up.

HARE winks at the audience. They exit, arm in arm.

The Strongest Person in the World

Based on a traditional story found in Japan, Korea and Europe.

Estimated running time: 10 minutes.

CAST: 6 (M) 2 (F)

Ratchel, *A teenage rat*

Scratchy, *Ratchel's cool friend*

Ma Rat, *Ratchel's mum*

Pa Rat, *Ratchel's dad*

Mr Sun

Mr Cloud

Mr Wind

Mr Wall

Director's Notes

There is plenty of fun to be had with this play. The rats make excellent characters to develop, while Sun, Cloud and Wind give you opportunities to experiment with dance, movement and costume design.

You will need: Rhythmic journey music[1]. A cymbal or gong. The costumes can be simple or elaborate - it's up to you!

 Tip:

Staging the Journey

Take time to experiment with the movement and dance sections in the play. Listening to different kinds of music can be inspiring. You can also try playing the game *Trickster* (p.15) as a way of coming up with ideas. You could set a journey theme before you start the game so that all the Leaders have to think of different ways of travelling when they are leading the movement. Soon you will have lots of suggestions to use.

As the rats go on their travels (p.47) make sure that different sections of the journey use mixed ways of moving and varying levels such as low, medium and high. Think about how you can show diverse landscapes and obstacles through mime and movement.

---

1 See www.dramaresource.com/playfulplays for suggested music tracks.

RATCHEL and SCRATCHY enter, playing a chasing game. SCRATCHY leapfrogs over RATCHEL.

MA RAT: *(Offstage)* Ratchel? Where are you?

RATCHEL: You'd better go, Scratchy!

SCRATCHY: Oh, alright. See you later.

SCRATCHY scratches himself, waves goodbye to RATCHEL and exits.

RATCHEL: I'm here, Mum.

MA RAT and PA RAT enter.

PA RAT: Who was that, Ratchel?

RATCHEL: No-one, Dad. Just a friend.

MA RAT: Ratchel, have you practised your tables today?

RATCHEL: Yes, Mum. I gnawed through a table leg this morning.

PA RAT: Good girl! What lovely sharp teeth you have.

RATCHEL: All the better to eat the piece of stinky cheese I found on the floor.

MA RAT: Good girl!

RATCHEL: It was covered in green mould and dog hairs.

PA RAT: Delicious! Did you save some for us?

RATCHEL: No, Dad, I ate it all up. Like a good girl.

PA AND MA: *(They smile at each other and say)* Good girl!

MA RAT: Off you go and play outside. Why don't you practise scurrying into dark holes?

RATCHEL: OK Mum! I'll go and look for some under the old wall.

              RATCHEL exits.

MA RAT: Ratchel is getting quite grown up now. I think it's time we found her a husband.

PA RAT: I'm sure that will be no problem. She has beautiful beady eyes, teeth as sharp as needles and a lovely long tail. She'll have young rats queuing up around the corner to be her husband.

MA RAT: *(Disappointed)* Young rats?

PA RAT: How about that friend of hers – Scratchy? He has such lovely long whiskers. He may be slightly spotty but he's very good at jumping onto tables at restaurants.

MA RAT: He's just an ordinary rat. A girl as beautiful and talented as Ratchel deserves someone better than that. She should marry the strongest person in the world.

PA RAT: The strongest person in the world? I think I know who that is.

MA RAT: Well, what are you waiting for? Let's go and see him. We'll take Ratchel with us.

PA RAT: Ratchel!

RATCHEL enters.

RATCHEL: Yes, Dad?

PA RAT: We're going on a journey!

RATCHEL: Where to?

PA RAT: To meet the strongest person in the world!

MUSIC: Rhythmic journey music. MA, PA and RATCHEL mime going on a long journey. Every now and then PA RAT points and they set off in a new direction. They get more and more tired until they finally arrive.

MUSIC stops. The RATS look around them.

RATCHEL: Wow! It's amazing!

MUSIC: Cymbal or gong. The SUN enters. The RATS bow to the SUN.

SUN: I call it the Golden Palace of the Sunset.

MA RAT: Mr Sun, we know that you give life and light to everything. You must be the strongest person in the world. This is our beautiful daughter, Ratchel. Would you marry her?

SUN: You are very kind to consider me as a husband.

RATCHEL: Wait a minute, Mum, you haven't asked me! Don't you think he's a bit too... hot for a husband?

MA RAT: But he's the strongest person in the world!

SUN: You are wrong. There is someone who is greater than me. He is so powerful that he can cover the whole sky and even make me disappear. Here he comes now!

MUSIC: Floaty music.

The CLOUD enters, dancing. He wears a cloak or holds a length of material. He dances across the stage and around the SUN, covering him up like a shadow. The SUN sinks and exits. The RATS bow to the CLOUD.

PA RAT: Mr Cloud, we know that you bring water to animals, plants and people. You are even mightier than the Sun. This is our beautiful daughter, Ratchel. Would you marry her?

MA RAT: What do you think, Ratchel?

RATCHEL: He just looks rather... fluffy.

CLOUD: Your daughter is indeed very beautiful, but I am not the strongest person in the world. There is one person who is greater than me. He is so powerful that he can catch me in his hands and throw me across the sky. Watch out, here he comes!

The WIND enters. He blows gently at the RATS and they take a few steps backwards. He blows hard at the CLOUD who twists and turns across and then off the stage. The RATS bow to the WIND.

MA RAT: Mr Wind, you carry ships across the seas and make hurricanes and tornados. You are stronger than Mr Cloud and more powerful than Mr Sun. This is our beautiful daughter, Ratchel. Would you marry her?

RATCHEL: No way! He's too full of hot air!

WIND: Sadly, your daughter is right. You may think I am powerful, but I am not the strongest person in the world. No matter how hard I blow, there is one person who can always stop me.

The WIND blows the RATS across and off the stage. The WALL enters. The RATS come back, blown by the wind. They fall down in front of the WALL. PA RAT gets up and bows to the WALL.

PA RAT: Mr Wall, you protect houses, towns and cities. You can even stop the Wind. You must be the strongest person in the world. This is our beautiful daughter, Ratchel. Would you marry her?

RATCHEL: A wall? You want me to marry an ugly old wall?

WALL: I understand that you don't want to marry me. It is true that I can stop the Wind, who can

blow the Cloud, who can cover the Sun. But even though I am very strong, there is one person who is even stronger than me. He is so powerful that he eats through me as though I'm made of cream cheese. When he digs beneath me with his mighty claws there is nothing I can do until I fall over.

RATS: *(All together)* Who is he?

WALL: He's a rat!

MA RAT: *(Surprised)* A rat?

PA RAT: Fancy that!

               SCRATCHY pops his head out from behind WALL. He steps out and stands in a cool pose.

SCRATCHY: And not just any rat! They call me... Scratchy!

               He scratches his bottom. RATCHEL steps forward shyly.

RATCHEL: Hello Scratchy! Are you really the strongest person in the world?

SCRATCHY: Maybe!

               SCRATCHY goes down on one knee.

SCRATCHY: Will you marry me?

RATCHEL: *(Thinks about it)* Yes, Scratchy, I will!

                RATCHEL and SCRATCHY hold hands. MA RAT and PA RAT smile at each other and clap their hands. All the actors enter.

                MUSIC: Lively music for a dance.

                RATCHEL and SCRATCHY lead the actors in a short celebratory dance. Finally everyone bows.

The Midas Touch

A Whoosh! storytelling performance based on the Greek Myth.

Estimated running time: 10 minutes.

CAST: 10-40 (M/F)

KING MIDAS

SILENUS, a satyr (half man, half goat)

SERVANTS

QUEEN

LITYERSES, Midas's son

DIONYSUS, a god

VARIOUS OBJECTS

Director's Notes

This is a play that requires no rehearsal. That's because it is a Whoosh! storytelling performance, where one person reads the story and everyone else steps into the space to instantly create characters, objects and locations. (See p.22 for full details.)

The story can be read aloud, or the storyteller can tell it in his or her own words. The words in CAPITALS indicate characters and objects to be created by the players. The words in the story which are spoken by the characters can be repeated by the actors.

I have suggested moments when the storyteller can say "Whoosh!", although of course it can be said at any time that the action in the circle gets too busy.

You will need: A small bell or triangle to ring when objects turn to gold. Choose one reliable player who would like to do this.

 Tip:

Instant Scenes

Warm up for this Whoosh! storytelling by playing *I Am A...* (p.20) or *Make Me A...* (p.21). These games will help the actors get used to creating scenes and objects very quickly so that they are ready to (literally) jump into the story.

Once upon a time in the sunny land of Greece lived a mighty KING, called King Midas. When the people of his country saw him they would bow down low. And he would wave to them.

(Encourage those in the circle to bow to the king.)

Most of his subjects thought he was a generous king, though some said he could be greedy.

One day King Midas was wandering through his garden. He walked between the TREES, with their leaves gently waving. He passed by the BUSHES and smelt the beautiful FLOWERS. The trees, bushes and flowers were all blowing gently in the breeze.

Suddenly King Midas heard a noise. A SATYR entered his garden. He had goat's legs and the head of a man. But he wasn't just any satyr, he was Silenus, chief of all the satyrs. He was tired from wandering in the hills and a little bit drunk.

"Would you like some breakfast?" asked King Midas. "Yes, please. I'm starving," replied Silenus. King Midas clicked his fingers and a SERVANT brought trays of fruit, bread and honey for Silenus to eat. Silenus gobbled it all up.

Silenus said, "That was delicious! In return for your kindness I will ask the god Dionysus to grant you a wish." "What can I wish for?" asked King Midas. "Anything at all," replied Silenus. You see, satyrs are friends of the gods. They are very magical.

King Midas pondered for a moment. Then he knew what he wanted. "I would like everything I touch to turn to gold," he said. "I don't think that's such a good idea," said Silenus. "Are you quite sure?" "Quite sure," said the king. "It is done," said Silenus and quick as a flash, he vanished. King Midas looked around his garden. He walked up to a tree and touched it. Immediately, it stopped blowing in the breeze and turned to gold.

(Play the bell sound each time King Midas turns an object into gold.)

"How wonderful! I'll soon be the richest king in the world," said King Midas. He went round his garden, touching everything in it – and soon he had turned it all to gold.

WHOOSH!

KING MIDAS went through the GRAND DOOR *(two children)* into his palace. As he walked through he touched the door and it turned into gold. He saw his dusty old palace in front of him – tall PILLARS, creaky DOORS, his THRONE, artistic STATUES and a big dining TABLE *(two children)*. He walked up to each object, touched it and soon his whole palace was gleaming bright gold.

King Midas sat on a CHAIR at the table and clicked his fingers. Two SERVANTS came running up to him. "More breakfast!" ordered the king, even though he had only just eaten. "And wine to drink!" he added.

The servants rushed around bringing food and drink to the table and soon there was a big feast laid before the king. The servants stepped back and watched and waited.

King Midas picked up a piece of bread. It turned to... gold. He picked up his glass of wine. The glass and the wine inside it turned into gleaming... gold. The grapes, bananas, cheese and meats, all turned to gold the moment he touched them. The king soon realised that he was unable to eat or drink.

At that moment, the QUEEN and Midas's SON came into the room. They looked about them in astonishment at the golden palace. The king's son ran up to him, saying "What's happened to the palace, Daddy?" He tried to hug Midas but as soon as he touched the king, he too was turned into... gold. A golden statue.

"Oh no, what have I done?" cried King Midas. He ran out of the room in horror.

WHOOSH!

KING MIDAS ran into his bedroom. He knelt down and prayed to his favourite god, Dionysus. "I have made a dreadful mistake. I was greedy and now everything I touch turns to gold, including my family. I can't even eat!"

DIONYSUS, god of grapes and wine, appeared before Midas in his bedroom. He was a kind and handsome god.

"We did warn you about your wish," said Dionysus. "But I can see that you have learned your lesson. Tomorrow you must go to the river and bathe. The curse will be lifted."

WHOOSH!

The next morning KING MIDAS went to the RIVER *(two or three children making waves)* and waded in. He washed himself and the water ran over him. When he stepped out, he noticed a FLOWER growing on the river bank. He touched it and… nothing happened! The spell had been washed away and all the sand on the river bed had turned to gold.

When Midas got home his SON came running towards him and everything had returned to normal. From that day on Midas chose to stop being greedy. He decided to live a quiet life in the country – but that's another story!

WHOOSH!

Why the Hippopotamus Wears No Coat

Based on a traditional story from Ghana.

Estimated running time: 10 minutes.

CAST: 4 - 10 or more (M/F)

NATURAL HISTORY TV PRESENTER

HIPPO

RAT

FIRE (DANCER)

FLAMES (DANCERS)

SINGERS

Director's Notes

The play can be performed by just four people (TV Presenter, Hippo, Rat and Fire) or several more can be added as dancers and singers. There are opportunities for audience participation in the play as they help Hippo to remember the rhyme and he looks amongst them for ingredients for his party.

You will need: A fur coat for Hippo (which certainly shouldn't be real fur) and a tail for Rat. Fire and the Flames need to be good at dancing or movement. Their costumes can be bright fiery colours and they can wave ribbons on sticks (like Chinese ribbon dancing) to provide flame effects. The TV Presenter can speak into a pretend microphone. The River can be created by two actors or stage-hands rippling some nice blue material or with painted cardboard.

 Tip:

Music

The music can be live, recorded or a mixture of the two. Some African music or drumming would be good for Fire and the Flames to dance to. I have written a tune for the song (with sheet music on p.71) and you can download a recording of this at www.dramaresource. com/playfulplays. Alternatively you can make up your own tune or simply chant the words.

The sound effects for the flickering flames can easily be made using maracas, shakers or dried peas in a plastic bottle.

The PRESENTER and HIPPO enter from opposite sides.

PRESENTER: The hippopotamus loves living in the water and is hardly ever out of it.

HIPPO mimes swimming and splashing in water.

His name means 'water horse'.

HIPPO raises his head to make a neighing noise.

But he's got nothing to do with horses. He's actually related to whales and porpoises.

HIPPO shrugs and swims again.

Once upon a time the hippopotamus lived on the land. He always wore a handsome coat of fur.

HIPPO swims to shore and puts on his fur coat.

You would often find him at home in his grass hut, admiring himself.

HIPPO preens himself before a mirror. RAT enters.

RAT: Good day, Hippo. Would you like to play a game with me?

HIPPO: *(Looking in the mirror and ignoring RAT.)* So soft. So shiny.

RAT: Did you hear me?

HIPPO: So smooth. So silky. So, so, so...

RAT: So beautiful?

HIPPO: Oh, hello, Rat. Do you really think so? You're not just saying that?

RAT: No, Hippo, I really do think you look... like a film star. Especially with your fashionable fur coat.

HIPPO: Well if you say so, Ratty. Do you think my fur coat is thicker than all of the other animals?

RAT: Without the shadow of a doubt, yours is the thickest of them all. Listen, Hippo. I can see that you're busy, but I'd really like it if you played a game of hide and seek with me.

HIPPO: Well... okay!

RAT: But you will be careful, won't you? You're a lot bigger than me.

HIPPO:

Yes, of course, don't worry. I'll hide first – you count.

RAT closes her eyes.

RAT:

One, two, three, four, five, six, seven, eight, nine, ten! Ready or not, here I come.

HIPPO hides but can clearly be seen. RAT pretends to look for him in all the wrong places until she eventually finds him.

Found you!

HIPPO:

Good hiding place, eh? I thought you'd never find me. Right-o – your turn.

RAT:

Close your eyes, then.

HIPPO:

Oh, sorry.

RAT:

And no peeping.

HIPPO:

Really, Ratty. As if I would. One, two, three, four…

RAT hides behind an object on stage, but her tail is sticking out. HIPPO finishes counting and starts looking around. He notices the mirror and looks into it. As he does so he accidentally treads on RAT's tail.

RAT: Ouch! That really hurts. Watch where you put your feet, big fella!

HIPPO: Whoops! I didn't mean to.

RAT: If only you paid more attention to your friends and less time to thinking about how nice you look!

HIPPO: Do you think I look nice? I mean – I'm really Ratty sorry. I mean, I'm really sorry Ratty. Really, it was an accident.

RAT: Huh! As if you care! *(Mutters.)* Accidentally on purpose, more like.

                RAT exits.

PRESENTER: Three days later…

HIPPO: *(Looking in the mirror.)* So soft. So shiny. So, so, so…

                Enter RAT.

RAT: So beautiful, Hippo. You look almost as beautiful as my friend, Fire.

HIPPO: What do you mean, almost as beautiful? Which friend? Who's Fire?

RAT: Oh, haven't you met Fire?

HIPPO: No, I don't think I have.

RAT: You like me, don't you Hippo?

HIPPO: Yes of course.

RAT: Well then, I bet you'd like my friend Fire.
               She's really hot!

HIPPO: Perhaps she would be friends with me too.
               Where does your friend Fire live?

RAT: Go over the mountain and through the trees,

               Cross the river and follow the breeze.

HIPPO: *(To himself)* Over the mountain and through
               the trees, cross the river and follow the
               breeze... *(To RAT)* Um, you'll have to go
               now, Ratty. I've just remembered there's
               somebody I have to visit. I've got to get
               ready.

               *RAT exits, looking secretly pleased. HIPPO
               preens himself once more.*

               Friend, indeed. I didn't know Ratty had
               any friends. Well, apart from me, of course.
               I wonder why I haven't met his friend Fire

before? I do hope Fire will like me. And if
Fire likes me, Ratty will like me even more.

HIPPO sets off on his journey.

HIPPO: Now, what did Ratty say?

*HIPPO encourages the audience to help him
remember the rhyme.*

(With the audience) Go over the... mountain
and through the... trees, cross the river and
follow... the breeze.

*MUSIC plays. HIPPO makes an imaginary
journey across and around the stage, miming
the mountain, the trees, the river and the breeze.
FIRE enters, bright and hot. She dances to the
music.*

You must be Fire! Delighted to make your
acquaintance. *(Indicating himself.)* Hippo.

*Journey MUSIC fades out or stops. Shakers or
other percussion instruments can be used to
illustrate FIRE's movements. HIPPO bows.
FIRE holds out her hand. HIPPO keeps his
distance.*

Um. No. I'd rather not shake hands just yet.
But I would like to get to know you a bit
more. Perhaps you'd like to visit my house.

FIRE is not so sure.

Believe me, we can be good friends. You will love my little grass hut.

FIRE flickers eagerly.

Please be my guest. You can come tomorrow afternoon. I'll prepare some food and we can play some silly party games.

FIRE nods and accepts. She exits and HIPPO returns home the way he came, dancing happily.

PRESENTER: The hippopotamus was so pleased, he couldn't stop dancing all the way home. He woke early the next day and went into the jungle looking for...

HIPPO looks amongst the audience, pretending to pick each ingredient from a different spectator.

...morning mushrooms... monkey nuts... bobbly berries... green guavas... and squishy bananas.

HIPPO chooses a member of the audience who is laughing to borrow the recipe from.

He borrowed a yummy recipe from his next-door neighbour, the laughing Hyena.

HIPPO mimes the cooking actions as they are narrated.

PRESENTER: He chopped, and stirred and cooked and tasted, then stood at the door of his house and waited.

MUSIC plays. FIRE and FLAMES enter and dance towards HIPPO.

SINGERS: Parrots squawking

Snakes are snaking

Monkeys swinging

Ground's a-shaking

Jungle smoking

Sparks are flying

Beasts have got no

Place to hide in

(Chorus)   *Fire's coming*

Coming through the jungle

Fire's coming

Coming through the jungle

Ants are marching

Lions roaring

Frogs are leaping

Vultures soaring

Branches blazing
Flames rise higher
Watch out, Hippo
Here comes Fire!

(Chorus)   *Fire's coming*
                 Coming through the jungle
                 Fire's coming
                 Coming through the jungle

                 Fire's coming
                 Coming through the jungle
                 Fire's coming
                 Coming through the jungle

                 FIRE and FLAMES get closer to HIPPO.

HIPPO: Oh no. Be careful Fire! Watch out for my little
                 grass hut!

                 The FLAMES reach HIPPO and take his fur
                 coat.

                 Oh no! You've taken my lovely fur coat!

                 HIPPO covers himself with his hands as though
                 he is naked. FIRE and the FLAMES exit.

HIPPO: Aaaaaarggh!

> *HIPPO runs towards the river and throws himself in. MUSIC: Splash sound. RAT appears on the bank.*

RAT: Hippo, I'm so sorry. I didn't expect all this to happen.

HIPPO: I'm never coming out again. Not without my fur coat. I'm so ashamed!

> *RAT exits sadly.*

PRESENTER: And from that day on, the 'water horse', or 'hippopotamus', wallowed in the mud and his fur coat was never seen again.

 Tip:

Free Download

On the facing page is the music for 'Fire's Coming'[1]. Visit the website to listen to and download a free audio file to sing along with in your production.
Go to: www.dramaresource.com/playfulplays

---

1 Thanks to Jonathan Lambert of www.lamsound.com for writing out the notation.

Fire's Coming
Words and Music by David Farmer

The Hungry Coat

Based on a traditional story from Aksehir, Turkey.

Estimated running time: 8-10 minutes.

CAST: 11-13 (M/F)

NASREDDIN

POSH LADY

POSH MAN

BOUNCER 1

BOUNCER 2

6-8 PARTY GOERS (They also play objects in NASREDDIN's house.)

Director's Notes

This play and the following one are based on stories about Nasreddin (also known as the 'Hodja'), a famous character in Turkish folk stories. He is one of those people who is said to be a "wise fool" (perhaps one modern equivalent is Mr Bean). In this play you can have fun experimenting with transitions between scenes. At one point the Party Guests freeze and become objects in Nasreddin's home. This is a quick way of moving from one location to another without any need for scenery or prop changes.

You will need: Essential for this play are a posh coat and a shabby-looking coat. The food can be mimed, otherwise it may get messy!

 Tip:

Transitions

To help with ideas for the scene which takes place in Nasreddin's house, play *Ten Second Objects* (p.17) or *I Am A....* (p.20). These drama games will help the actors get used to creating objects quickly. Once you have decided how to create the objects you need, practise moving from a freeze-frame at the party to Nasreddin's house as smoothly as possible. It may help if you play some magical-sounding music to get the actors into the mood.

Scene One: *A Street in the Town.*

POSH LADY: How exciting! It's Abdullah's birthday party
                tonight!

POSH MAN: He always has the liveliest party in town.

POSH LADY: And the most delicious feast!

POSH MAN: All the smartest people will be there.

POSH LADY: Like you and me! *(They laugh loudly.)*

                NASREDDIN enters, wearing a shabby-looking
                coat. The POSH LADY and POSH MAN give
                each other a funny look and hold their noses.

POSH MAN: We'd better not be late.

NASREDDIN: Excuse me, are you going to Abdullah's
                party?

POSH LADY: We might be.

NASREDDIN: Me too!

POSH MAN: Really? You can only go if you have a proper
                invitation.

                The POSH LADY and POSH MAN exit.

NASREDDIN: *(Imitating the POSH MAN)* You can only go if
              you have a proper invitation. *(As himself)* Oh
              well, I'd better go on my own. I don't want
              to miss the feast, I'm starving.

              NASREDDIN follows them off.

Scene Two: Outside the Party.

              *Party music plays from inside the house. The
              BOUNCERS enter.*

BOUNCER 1:   *(Yawns.)* I think it's going to be a lively night.

BOUNCER 2:   Could be. We'd better keep an eye out for
              trouble-makers.

              They crack their knuckles. NASREDDIN enters.

BOUNCER 1:   *(Blocking the way.)* 'Ere, where do you think
              you're going?

NASREDDIN: To Abdullah's feast.

BOUNCER 2:   Not without a proper invitation, you're not
              going nowhere.

NASREDDIN: I see.

              *NASREDDIN starts searching through his
              pockets. He pulls out a bus ticket, an apple core*

and a few other strange items. The BOUNCERS
are not amused.

BOUNCER 1: Come on, we haven't got all night.

NASREDDIN pulls out a screwed-up invitation
from his back pocket. He carefully unfolds it
and gives it to BOUNCER 1, who looks at it
suspiciously and then shows it to BOUNCER 2.
The BOUNCERS nod to each other.

BOUNCER 2: Mmmm, well it is a proper invitation.

BOUNCER !: I suppose we'd better let him in.

The BOUNCERS mime opening some doors and
then exit.

Scene Three: At the Party.

Immediately the music gets louder to indicate
that NASREDDIN has arrived at the party.
Several PARTY GOERS enter, dancing to the
music. NASREDDIN starts to dance but the
PARTY GOERS ignore him and smile at each
other to show they are having a good time.

NASREDDIN: *(To PARTY GOER 1.)* Good evening, it's a
fabulous party, isn't it?

PARTY GOER 1: *(Ignoring him.)* Oh I say, look who is over
there! Princess Yasemin!

NASREDDIN: I'm sure I've met you somewhere before.

PARTY GOER 1:   She's so famous and adorable. I simply must go and talk to her.

PARTY GOER 1 waves to another PARTY GOER, crosses over and has a mimed conversation.

NASREDDIN: *(To PARTY GOER 2.)* Hello, it's a lovely evening. Are you enjoying yourself?

PARTY GOER 2:   *(Ignoring him.)* There's a strange smell round here.

NASREDDIN: Would you like to hear a really funny joke?

PARTY GOER 2:   Oh look over there – isn't that the Grand Vizier?

NASREDDIN: Why did the donkey get married?

PARTY GOER 2:   *(Interrupting.)* The Grand Vizier! He's so famous! I simply must go and talk to him.

PARTY GOER 2 waves and crosses to have a mimed conversation with another PARTY GOER.

NASREDDIN: *(Shouts to PARTY GOER 2)* So she could wear a twenty-four carrot ring!

The music stops and the PARTY GOERS freeze.

NASREDDIN: *(To the audience.)* They're just ignoring me. How dare they! Just because I have the dust of the road on my clothes. I have had enough of this treatment!

(NASREDDIN exits.)

Scene Three: Nasreddin's House.

Magical music plays. The PARTY GOERS change positions in slow-motion to make the shape of objects in NASREDDIN's house – a DOOR, a SHOWER, a MIRROR, a WARDROBE and one actor plays a DONKEY outside the house. When the actors are in position the music fades out and NASREDDIN enters.

NASREDDIN: Home sweet home!

The DONKEY brays and NASREDDIN pats it gently.

NASREDDIN: Are you pleased to see me?

The DONKEY nods and brays. NASREDDIN opens the creaky DOOR and enters his house. He takes off his coat and puts it in the WARDROBE, who holds it for him. He pretends to get undressed and stands underneath the SHOWER. He turns the tap and the SHOWER comes to life with sounds and action. NASREDDIN washes himself and turns off the SHOWER. He dries himself with an imaginary towel and then looks in the MIRROR. Every movement he makes is copied by the MIRROR. He makes a face at it and a few other movements and then carefully combs his hair. He speaks and the MIRROR speaks at the same time.

NASREDDIN:
and   There, that's better. Clean and tidy.
MIRROR:

NASREDDIN steps away from the MIRROR and goes to the WARDROBE.

NASREDDIN: Now, what shall I wear?

NASREDDIN opens the wardrobe and mimes putting on trousers and shirt.

NASREDDIN: A nice clean shirt and smart trousers.

NASREDDIN looks at the coat which he put in the WARDROBE earlier on.

NASREDDIN: I can't wear this coat. It's too old and dirty. Where is my smart one?

One of the actors playing the WARDROBE speaks.

WARDROBE: Hold on a minute.

The WARDROBE actor takes the old coat and goes off-stage. The actor quickly returns with a much smarter coat and gives it to NASREDDIN, then becomes part of the WARDROBE again.

NASREDDIN: Ah, here it is!

NASREDDIN puts on his smart coat. The magical music plays and all the actors exit, apart from NASREDDIN. The music fades out. NASREDDIN fastens the final button on his coat, smiles at the audience and exits confidently.

Scene Four: Back at the Party.

The BOUNCERS enter and the party music plays quietly.

BOUNCER 1:   I must say, it has been a busy night.

BOUNCER 2:   And the party is still in full swing.

BOUNCER 1:   We'd better keep an eye out for trouble-makers, just in case.

NASREDDIN enters.

BOUNCER 2:   Well, good evening Sir!

NASREDDIN: Shall I go round the back?

BOUNCER 1:   No need for that, Sir. *(Loudly.)* The most venerable Nasreddin has arrived!

The BOUNCERS exit. The music increases in volume. Enter the PARTY GOERS, carrying plates and bowls.

PARTY GOER 1: Oh I say, look who it is!

PARTY GOER 2: Oh Nasreddin, you do look wonderful.

PARTY GOER 1: How wonderful to see you.

PARTY GOER 2: Awesome. It's awesome to see you.

NASREDDIN: Funny you didn't see me before.

PARTY GOER 3: Do have some spicy lentil soup.

NASREDDIN: *(Dipping his coat into the food.)* Eat, my lovely coat, eat!

PARTY GOER 4: Please help yourself to stuffed vine leaves.

NASREDDIN: *(Putting the food into his pockets.)* Eat, my lovely coat, eat!

PARTY GOER 5: Why not try some delicious figs?

NASREDDIN: *(Rubbing the food into his coat.)* Eat, my lovely coat, eat!

PARTY GOER 6: Do have some freshly-baked baklava.

NASREDDIN: *(Pouring the food over his coat.)* Eat, my lovely
                     coat, eat!

PARTY GOER 1: Esteemed Nasreddin, why don't *you* eat the
                     food?

NASREDDIN: There's no point in eating it myself.

PARTY GOER 2: Why not?

NASREDDIN: When I arrived in my old clothes, nobody
                     wanted to know me. Now I wear my posh
                     coat, nothing seems too good for me. That
                     proves it was the coat, not me, that was
                     invited to the feast. If you think my coat is
                     so wonderful, then it may as well eat all the
                     food!

                     The PARTY GOERS look shocked.

NASREDDIN: Goodbye!

                     NASREDDIN exits.

The Talking Donkey

Based on a traditional story from Aksehir, Turkey.

Estimated running time: 5 minutes.

CAST: 6-16 (M/F)

Aziz, *a donkey vendor*

Nasreddin

Mustafa, *a thief*

Hasan, *Mustafa's friend*

Shoppers

Stall holders

Donkeys

Director's Notes

This play is based on another of the famous Turkish fables about the wise fool Nasreddin Hodja.

You will need: As there are donkeys in the play (as well as a man who pretends to be a donkey), it is useful to make some masks or donkey ears so that the audience always knows who's who! Don't forget that one donkey needs longer ears than the others. It's also good fun to add hoof sound effects using coconut shells.

 Tip:

Crowd Scenes

If you want to involve more actors then cast them as shoppers, donkeys and other characters in the market. Take time building up the market scene at the beginning and end. Even in a crowd scene each character should know why they are there - it's not enough to have a few people wandering around saying "rhubarb"! See how many different kinds of crowd characters you can come up with.

Scene One: *Market day.*

A few SHOPPERS, including MUSTAFA and HASAN, are walking through the market visiting the STALL HOLDERS. AZIZ enters, leading some DONKEYS. They make occasional braying sounds.

AZIZ: Donkeys for sale! Get your donkey here! Pull your cart! Plough your field! Free bag of carrots!

One or two of the SHOPPERS look at the DONKEYS, stroking and patting them or looking at their teeth. NASREDDIN enters, carrying a big bag.

AZIZ: Good afternoon, sir. It looks like you've bought a lot today.

NASREDDIN: Yes, enough for a hearty meal. Onions, tomatoes, peppers, potatoes, bread, rice, melons....

The SHOPPERS exit, apart from MUSTAFA and HASAN who quietly watch AZIZ and NASREDDIN.

AZIZ: Have you got far to travel? Your bag looks very heavy!

NASREDDIN: It is quite a long way. About three hours'

walk to my village.

AZIZ: Just imagine if you had a strong donkey to carry your bag home for you!

NASREDDIN: That would be very nice. But I don't think I could afford one of your donkeys.

AZIZ: You'd be surprised! How much money have you got?

NASREDDIN: Well...

NASREDDIN takes out his purse. AZIZ takes it and looks inside.

AZIZ: You're Nasreddin, right?

NASREDDIN: That's my name.

AZIZ: You're well-known around this town. Many say you are a wise man.

MUSTAFA and HASAN whisper to each other and giggle.

AZIZ: For you we have a special price. *(Looks in the purse again.)* In fact, you have just the right amount in your purse. Would you like to take one now?

NASREDDIN: Really? That's very kind of you. May I have
              that one? The one with the long ears.

              NASREDDIN points at one of the DONKEYS.
              AZIZ nods and NASREDDIN puts his bag over
              the back of the DONKEY. He pulls on the rope
              but the donkey doesn't move.

DONKEY: Ee-aw! Ee-aw!

AZIZ: Don't forget your free bag of carrots!

              AZIZ gives NASREDDIN a bag of carrots.
              NASREDDIN holds one in front of the donkey
              and it follows him off stage. MUSTAFA and
              HASAN whisper to each other and nod, then
              follow NASREDDIN.

Scene Two: *A Mountain Path.*

              NASREDDIN enters, leading the DONKEY on a
              journey around and across the stage. MUSTAFA
              and HASAN enter. They are secretly trying
              to steal the DONKEY. Eventually HASAN
              whispers to MUSTAFA, who pulls the rope off
              the donkey and puts it round HASAN's neck. He
              also puts the bag on HASAN's back. MUSTAFA
              produces a carrot and leads the DONKEY off-
              stage. NASREDDIN continues on his journey
              without realising what has happened. HASAN
              walks normally (on two legs). NASREDDIN
              passes a carrot behind him without looking.
              HASAN takes it from him and takes a bite out of
              it.

HASAN: Ee-aw! Ee-aw!

NASREDDIN: Don't worry, Donkey. Not far to go now!

                They exit. A few moments later they enter again.

Scene Three: *Nasreddin's House.*

NASREDDIN: Here we are! Home sweet home! I've only got one carrot left but you can have it as a reward for carrying my heavy bag.

HASAN: Thank you, Nasreddin.

NASREDDIN: You - you can speak!

                NASREDDIN turns around in shock.

NASREDDIN: You're a man, not a donkey!

HASAN: It's true.

NASREDDIN: Where is my donkey? What have you done with him?

HASAN: I am truly sorry. You see, my mother has magical powers. Yesterday I spoke to her very rudely. I regret what I said. But it was too late – she turned me into a donkey as punishment and sold me at the market.

NASREDDIN: But how did you change back into a man?

HASAN: My mother promised that if a good man bought me, I would change back. You paid for me, so you must be a good man. Thank you so much!

NASREDDIN unties HASAN.

NASREDDIN: Just go home. And promise me you will never say a bad thing to your mother again.

HASAN: I promise. Goodbye. Thank you, once more.

HASAN exits.

NASREDDIN: *(Grumbling to himself.)* What a waste of money. I shall have to buy another donkey.

NASREDDIN exits.

Scene Four: *The Next Day at the Market.*

SHOPPERS and STALL HOLDERS enter. AZIZ enters, leading some donkeys. One of them is the same one that NASREDDIN bought previously.

AZIZ: Donkeys for sale! Get your donkey here! Pull your cart! Plough your field! Free bag of carrots!

NASREDDIN enters. He sees the DONKEYS and goes over to them. He looks curiously at the donkey with the long ears. He waits until AZIZ is looking the other way then leans down and talks to it.

NASREDDIN: I told you to be polite to your mother! I can see what she's done to you.

The DONKEY looks curiously at NASREDDIN. AZIZ looks curiously at NASREDDIN, who smiles back at him.

NASREDDIN: *(To Aziz.)* I have decided not to buy this donkey today, thank you. Once was enough. *(Whispering into the donkey's ear.)* I hope you learn your lesson this time. Goodbye!

NASREDDIN exits. AZIZ shrugs his shoulders and pats the DONKEY. AZIZ leads the donkeys away, calling out as he does so.

AZIZ: Donkeys for sale! Get your donkey here! Free bag of carrots!

The Musicians of Bremen

Based on a story from the Brothers Grimm.

Estimated running time: 12-15 minutes.

CAST: 9 (M/F)

DONKEY

DOG

CAT

ROOSTER

ROBBER 1: FIDDLESTICKS

ROBBER 2: TRICKSY

ROBBER 3: SNITCH

ROBBER 4: MUGGINS

TREE

Director's Notes

This is the longest play in this volume. You will need more rehearsal time and to make sure that everyone keeps practising their lines (don't forget the tips on pages 28-9). The play gives the cast and director opportunities to have fun with the characters, action sequences and songs.

You will need: Half-masks to cover the eyes and nose would be good for the animal characters, or you might like to experiment with face make-up and some colourful costumes.

 Tip:

Developing Characters

There are two main groups of characters - the animals and the robbers. Take time to explore each character using some of the ideas on pages 24-6. Remember the animals are quite old so think about how to use your voices and bodies to show that.

All the characters can be played by boys or girls, so you may sometimes need to change "he" to "she" or the other way round.

DONKEY enters slowly carrying a sack of corn on his back. The following can be sung to the tune of 'Clementine'.

DONKEY: I'm a donkey

In the farmyard

And I used to be the best.

But I'm old now

And I'm wonky

And it's time to have a rest.

DONKEY puts down his sack and sits on it.

FARMER: *(Offstage.)* Donkey! Have you finished that job yet?

DONKEY: I'd better carry this sack in,

Or I'll get a whacking!

DONKEY tries to carry the sack but stumbles. He looks at audience for sympathy. Brays.

Ee-aw, ee-aw, ee-aw.

FARMER enters.

FARMER: Come on you lazy good-for-nothing donkey!

DONKEY struggles with the sack and then drops it on the ground.

DONKEY: Ee-aw. Ee-aw.

FARMER: I'm fed up with you! I'm going home for a cup of tea. By the time I come back, I expect you to have moved all fifty sacks of corn. Or else...

FARMER makes a throat cutting sign and exits. DONKEY looks at audience and gulps loudly.

DONKEY: What am I to do? I've been carrying sacks of corn my whole life. I can't help it if I'm old. I'm doing my best! And now he says...

DONKEY holds his throat and gulps.

DONKEY: At my age I should be munching away in a field of delicious green grass, not working like a slave. When I was young I used to dream of being a rock star. That's it! I'll run away to Bremen Town, to busk in the streets. Goodbye Farmer and goodbye corn!

DONKEY kicks the sack of corn off stage and goes off in the opposite direction. DOG runs on and pants. He looks behind him.

DOG: That's far enough. Hopefully, my nasty master won't bother looking for me now.

(Listens.) Oops! Too late, I think I can hear him coming.

DOG pretends to be a tree, but he is still panting. DONKEY enters. DOG holds his breath. DONKEY walks past the tree then looks at it in a puzzled way. Eventually DOG has to start breathing again. He stops pretending to be a tree.

DONKEY: Why were you pretending to be a tree? And why are you out of breath?

DOG: *(Panting.)* I've been running all morning - running away from my nasty master. I thought you were him. He says I'm too old to hunt any more.

DONKEY: And are you?

DOG: Well, I think I'm losing my sense of smell. Last time he sent me off to collect a duck, I came back with a cheese and pickle sandwich.

DONKEY: Well at least it was something to eat.

DOG: *(Whispers.)* He said he was going to…

               DOG makes throat-cutting sign. Both animals gulp.

DONKEY: My master is just as bad. He wants to do the same to me. So I'm going to Bremen Town to become a busker. In fact, I'm looking for animals to join my band. You don't know any drummers, do you?

DOG: Well, actually…

               MUSIC: A drum solo. DOG mimes playing the drums.

DONKEY: Hey, that's not bad. Why don't you come with me? You know what they say? Two's company!

DOG: I don't mind if I doooooo-oo! *(DOG howls the last word like a wolf.)*

               DONKEY and DOG exit. CAT enters from the opposite side, looking very sad.

CAT: *(Walks mournfully about the stage.)* Mia-oooow! Mia-oooow! Mia-oooow!

DOG and DONKEY enter and watch CAT.

CAT: *(Miserably.)* Mia-oooow!

DOG: What's this? A furry lump of grumps?

DONKEY: Why are you so down in the dumps?

DOG: What's the matter, catter?

CAT: *(Looking warily at the DOG.)* Matter? How dare you ask me what the matter is!

DOG: *(Growls half-heartedly)* Don't worry, I'm too old and slow to chase you.

DONKEY: We just want to help you. I'm a donkey, by the way, in case you couldn't tell.

CAT: Well, if you really want to know, I'm miserable because my mistress tried to drown me.

DONKEY: Did you do something wrong?

CAT: It's what I didn't do that's the problem! She wants me to chase the mice. But I'm too old for all that now. They run circles around me. I'm much happier when I'm having a doze next to the nice warm stove.

DONKEY: So why have you come to the forest?

CAT: That mischievous mistress chased me with her broom down to the river and threw me in. I'm allergic to water but luckily I landed on a log and floated away. I ended up here, in the forest.

DOG: Well, maybe you should come with us. We're going to form a band.

CAT: Cool.

DONKEY: Are you any good at singing? I know a lot of cool cats that like to sing all night long.

CAT: *(Modestly)* Well, as it happens, I do know one or two serenades. *(Miaows painfully.)* Have you got any gigs lined up?

DONKEY: Not exactly. But we're going to try – in Bremen Town.

CAT: Count me in! It sounds just purr-fect.

The three animals exit. Enter ROOSTER, who starts to anxiously crow and strut around.

ROOSTER: *(Said as a rap.)* Cock-a-doodle-doo! Cock-a-doodle-doo!   Cock-a-doodle-oodle-oodle-oodle-oodle-doo!

CAT, DOG and DONKEY enter and watch ROOSTER, who hasn't seen them yet. They look quite worried.

ROOSTER: Cock-a-doodle-doo! Cock-a-doodle-doo! Cock-a-doodle –

DOG: (Interrupting) – Don't! I think we get the picture.

DONKEY: (To ROOSTER.) It's way past dawn. Why are you still cock-a-doodle-doing?

ROOSTER: I woke up everybody on the farm this morning to tell them the sun was shining brightly. But instead of thanking me, I heard my monstrous mistress say to the cook that she plans to cut off my head tomorrow and serve me up for Sunday lunch! That's why I'm still crowing. I won't get another chance to crow after today. Cock-a-doodle…

CAT: (Interrupting.) Why don't you cock-a-doodle come with us? We're all escaping from our masters and mistresses. We're going to Bremen Town to play music in the streets.

DOG: Would you like to join our band?

ROOSTER: Anything to get away from this farm! And as you can tell I happen to be quite good at rapping. Yo!

CAT: Now our band is big enough to put on a concert, we're going to need a name.

DOG: How about 'The Beastles?'[1]

CAT: It's been done, I think. What do you think of 'Party Animals'?

DOG: That's not bad... for a cat.

DONKEY: I think we should stop talking and look for somewhere to sleep. We'll never make it to Bremen Town before it gets dark.

ROOSTER: I know - 'Farmyard Frenzy'!

CAT
&
DOG: I like it!

DONKEY: Come on! Hurry up!

The four ANIMALS exit. Enter the four ROBBERS. They sit down on chairs on one side of the stage (they can bring these on if necessary).

FIDDLE: Right, Tricksy, let's go over the plan one more time shall we?

---

1 Yes, there is supposed to be an 'S' in the middle!

TRICKSY: *(Pointing to MUGGINS.)* Muggins, you are going to be up on the roof keeping an eye out in case anybody comes along.

SNITCH: The three of us – Fiddlesticks, Tricksy and me – will be inside the house looking for jewellery and other valuables.

MUGGINS: Come on Snitch, that's not fair! What if it's raining?

TRICKSY: Take an umbrella. *(She laughs.)*

MUGGINS: I always have to be the one that waits outside.

FIDDLE: That's because *we* know exactly what we're looking for.

MUGGINS: I'm just saying, I think somebody else should have a turn sometimes.

SNITCH: Never mind that, Muggins, let's have something to eat. I don't like to rob on an empty stomach.

They mime eating and drinking a hearty meal. TREE enters on the opposite side.

TREE: *(To the audience.)* I'm a tree. A real one!

The four ANIMALS enter and stop near the TREE as though they haven't seen the house.

DONKEY: I'm so tired. This handy tree will make a great place to rest. *(Lies down and yawns.)*

DOG: I'm going to sleep with Donkey at the bottom of the tree. If anyone comes along I'll bite them and send them on their way.

CAT: I'm going to climb up a little bit. I feel safer sleeping in the branches.

CAT pretends to climb TREE, looks over one of the branches and falls asleep.

ROOSTER: *(Whispering.)* And I'll climb up to the very top. That's where I usually sleep.

ROOSTER pretends to climb to the top. He looks around and then notices the ROBBERS in their house.

ROOSTER: I can see a light in a house. It's not very far away.

DONKEY: We should go there and see if there's a warm place to sleep. It's not very comfortable sleeping on twigs and fir cones.

DOG: Maybe there will be a bone or two to eat. I'm starving!

They all creep across the stage. Whenever the ROBBERS speak the ANIMALS freeze in position (like Grandma's Footsteps).

TRICKSY: This meat is delicious!

DOG licks his lips. The ROBBERS continue to eat for a few moments and the ANIMALS start creeping again until SNITCH speaks.

SNITCH: *(To FIDDLESTICKS.)* Pass me the salt and pepper will you? I want to put some on this fish.

CAT licks her lips. The ROBBERS eat and drink and the ANIMALS creep until they are next to the house, unseen by the ROBBERS.

MUGGINS: *(To SNITCH.)* Pass me the carrots. Please?

DONKEY licks his lips.

MUGGINS: I think they'll go well with this chicken.

ROOSTER looks appalled.

CAT: We need a plan!

DOG: Maybe if we sing them a song they'll give us something to eat.

ROOSTER: But if we're going to sing to them we need to be able to see our audience.

DONKEY: Good point. Dog, climb onto my back.

The ANIMALS pretend to climb onto each other's shoulders. This can be done by DONKEY kneeling down and the others holding their heads one by one above DONKEY's head so that the audience see four faces in a column.

DOG: Climb up, Cat!

CAT places her head above DOG's.

CAT: Come on, Rooster!

ROOSTER places his head above CAT's.

ROOSTER: After three – one, two, three!

The ANIMALS start singing loudly at the same time – braying, barking, meowing and crowing. The ROBBERS stop eating as they hear the noise. They look over at the ANIMALS in shock and fear for several seconds. Suddenly the ANIMALS start to wobble and fall forward into the house, still making their sounds. They scatter the ROBBERS, who look as though they have seen a ghost and run out of the house and exit.

DONKEY: Well, that seemed to work!

DOG: In a way.

                 The ANIMALS look at the food and start eating hungrily.

CAT: It's delicious.

DONKEY: Pass me the carrots. Please?

ALL: Yum, yum, yum!

                 Eventually they stop eating and look tired.

ROOSTER: Time for bed.

CAT: I'm going to sleep in this warm spot by the fireplace.

DOG: I'll guard the door.

ROOSTER: I'll have a snooze in the rafters. *(This can be on a chair or stage block.)*

DONKEY: I think I saw some hay in the yard. I'll sleep there. Good night!

ANIMALS: Good night!

The ANIMALS fall asleep. The ROBBERS enter, acting as though they can't see anything.

FIDDLE: *(Whispering.)* It was most definitely a hobgoblin.

TRICKSY: No, a hobgoblin doesn't make those barking noises. It was a bogeyman.

SNITCH: If you ask me it was a flibbertigibbet!

MUGGINS: Listen – I think it's gone to sleep.

They all listen. The ANIMALS are making various types of snoring sounds.

FIDDLE: How can you tell?

MUGGINS: Listen to it snoring!

TRICKSY: I think you'd better go and check.

MUGGINS: What?

SNITCH: Maybe you can catch it.

MUGGINS: Why does it always have to be me?

FIDDLE: It just does!

MUGGINS is shoved by the other three ROBBERS towards the house. He creeps up slowly and goes in.

MUGGINS: *(Whispering.)* I can't see anything. It's dark!

TRICKSY: Light a candle!

MUGGINS takes a candle out of his pocket but he hasn't got a match. He looks around for one. CAT opens her eyes wide and watches him.

MUGGINS: Ooh look, two bright coals. I could light my candle on them.

MUGGINS goes towards CAT and holds the candle towards her. CAT meows loudly, spits at him and scratches him with her paw. The other ANIMALS wake up. MUGGINS is so frightened that he runs towards the door where DOG is sleeping. DOG bites MUGGINS on the leg. MUGGINS passes near to DONKEY who kicks him.

ROOSTER: Cock-a-doodle-doo! Cock-a-doodle-doo!
Cock-a-doodle-oodle-oodle-oodle-oodle-doo!

MUGGINS runs back to the other ROBBERS.

ROBBERS: What happened?

MUGGINS: A witch with eyes of fire scratched me
with her bony fingers. Then a fiendish ogre
stabbed me with his dagger and a giant
walloped me with a club. And on top of the
house, was the very Devil himself, calling
out "I'll come and get you, I'll come and get
you."

*The ROBBERS look at each other and then run
off stage in terror. The ANIMALS smile at each
other.*

DONKEY: Friends, I think we have found ourselves a
new home to live in. We never need to work
again.

CAT: We can just make music all day long!

ANIMALS: Whoopee!

*The ANIMALS sing a song and dance to the tune
of 'For He's A Jolly Good Fellow.'*

ANIMALS: We frightened off the robbers
            We frightened off the robbers
            We frightened off the robbers
            And now we all live here
            And now we all live here
            And now we all live here
            We're braver than the bravest
            We're braver than the bravest
            We're braver than the bravest
            And now we all live here!

Stone Soup

Based on a traditional story found across Europe.

Estimated running time: 6-8 minutes.

CAST: 6-30 M/F

THREE SOLDIERS

THREE NEIGHBOURS

VILLAGERS

Director's Notes

The play can be performed by a small cast of half a dozen or a whole class, as you can have as many villagers as you like and maybe some extra soldiers. Just share the lines out. You could perform this play as a way of celebrating the harvest festival. Take your time with the section where the villagers are bringing lots of ingredients and setting the tablecloth for the feast.

You will need: A nice big cauldron or soup pot with a large spoon will provide a focus for the action. The ingredients can be real or simply painted on card. You will also need to make some special hats (see below).

 Tip:

The Neighbours

Each NEIGHBOUR represents both a person and a house. One way to do this is for the actors to wear a hat shaped like the roof of a house. This could have a cardboard door coming down over the actor's face like a mask, or the actor could hold a cardboard cut-out of a door in front of his or her face. Another very simple solution is for the characters to simply hold up their hands like pages of a book in front of their faces. When the soldiers knock at their houses they can open the door (or their hands) to look out.

Scene One:	*Somewhere in the countryside.*
	Three tired-looking SOLDIERS wearing rucksacks march on and face the audience. They continue marching on the spot.
SOLDIER 1:	I'm starving.
SOLDIER 2:	It's two days since our last breakfast.
SOLDIER 3:	I'm so hungry I could eat that stone! At least it would fill the hole in my belly.
	SOLDIER 3 picks up a stone and is going to put it in his mouth.
SOLDIER 1:	No, don't do that!
	SOLDIER 3 stops and looks at the stone he is holding.
SOLDIER 3:	Why not?
SOLDIER 1:	There's a village ahead.
SOLDIER 2:	Maybe they'll have some food.
SOLDIER 3:	Right turn!

They march off. SOLDIER 3 still has the stone.

Scene Two: *In the village.*

Enter three NEIGHBOURS who stand in a row. The SOLDIERS enter.

SOLDIER 2:   That's strange! There's no-one around.

SOLDIER 1:   Maybe nobody lives here any more.

SOLDIER 3:   Let's find out!

SOLDIER 3 goes to the first house and knocks on the door (with appropriate sound effects).

SOLDIER 3:   Anybody home?

NEIGHBOUR 1: No!

SOLDIER 3:   *(To the other SOLDIERS.)* That's a shame.

SOLDIER 2:   Try again. I'm sure I heard something.

SOLDIER 3:   *(Knocks and speaks more loudly.)* Anyone home?

NEIGHBOUR 1: *(Opens the door and looks out grumpily.)* What do you want?

SOLDIER 3:   We're three hungry soldiers. Have you got any food to spare?

NEIGHBOUR 1:   Food? To spare? No way!

NEIGHBOUR 1 closes the door. The SOLDIERS look at each other and shrug their shoulders. They move onto the next house.

SOLDIER 2:   *(Knocks.)* Anybody home?

NEIGHBOUR 2:   *(With door closed.)* What do you want?

SOLDIER 2:   We're very hungry. Have you got any spare food? Maybe a carrot?

NEIGHBOUR 2:   A carrot? There are eleven of us in this family. We hardly have enough to feed ourselves!

The SOLDIERS shrug their shoulders. Behind their backs NEIGHBOUR 2 opens the door and looks out suspiciously.

SOLDIER 1:   *(Sighs.)* Let's try the next one.

NEIGHBOUR 2 closes the door before the SOLDIERS see her. SOLDIER 1 goes to the next house and knocks on the door.

SOLDIER 1:   We're tired and hungry. Have you got a crust of bread to spare?

NEIGHBOUR 3:   *(Opens the door.)* Bread? You've got to be joking. We had a terrible harvest this year. There's none left!

> *NEIGHBOUR 3 closes the door. The soldiers look at each other and then come together to whisper. The three NEIGHBOURS open their doors and try to listen. SOLDIER 3 shows his stone to the other SOLDIERS.*

SOLDIER 1:   *(Loudly.)* These poor villagers have no food to spare. We'll have to make some stone soup!

> *The SOLDIERS gather wood for a fire. The NEIGHBOURS in their houses look puzzled. Several VILLAGERS enter from the sides. They watch the soldiers suspiciously.*

VILLAGER 1:   What are you doing?

SOLDIER 2:   We're making stone soup! Has anyone got a big pot we could use?

> *Two of the VILLAGERS nod at each other. They exit.*

SOLDIER 3:   And we'll need some water – lots of it!

VILLAGER 2:   I suppose we could bring you some from the well.

VILLAGER 2 nods at another VILLAGER and they exit. The SOLDIERS rub two sticks together to light a fire. The fire lights and the SOLDIERS warm their hands. Two VILLAGERS return with a large cooking pot which is placed on the fire. Two more VILLAGERS return with jugs of water which the SOLDIERS pour into their pot. The water can be mimed.

SOLDIER 3:   *(Dropping the stone into the pot.)* This will be delicious!

SOLDIER 1:   *(Looking round at the VILLAGERS.)* We should have enough to share with everyone!

SOLDIER 2:   *(Stirring the soup with a wooden spoon.)* This soup would be even more delicious if we had a little onion or garlic.

The VILLAGERS look at each other. Two of them step forward.

VILLAGER 3:   I might have an onion at the back of my cupboard.

VILLAGER 4:   And I may have a few cloves of garlic.

The two VILLAGERS go off.

SOLDIER 1:   *(Loudly.)* You know what makes stone soup even more delicious? Carrots...

SOLDIER 2:   … and cabbage…

SOLDIER 3:   … and a dash of salt and pepper!

> *Three of the VILLAGERS look at each other, nod and exit. Two VILLAGERS return with onions and garlic which they give to the soldiers. The NEIGHBOURS are still watching.*

VILLAGER 3:   This should add some flavour!

> *The SOLDIERS add the vegetables to the pot and stir it. The other VILLAGERS return with carrots, cabbage, salt and pepper, which are added to the pot.*

SOLDIER 2:   It's starting to smell good.

SOLDIER 3:   I wonder what else we could add to it?

> *Music: Celebratory music plays.*
> *The VILLAGERS talk amongst themselves. Several of them exit and return with different ingredients, such as beans, vegetables, plastic bones, toy sausages and so on. Even the NEIGHBOURS (still wearing their hats) bring some offerings. Everything is added to the pot. The SOLDIERS thank everyone and continue to stir the soup and blow on the fire. Some VILLAGERS bring on a tablecloth, which can be spread on the ground or on a small table.*

SOLDIERS: *(Together.)* It's ready!

The VILLAGERS and NEIGHBOURS line up and hold mimed soup bowls. The SOLDIERS ladle soup into the bowls. Everyone gathers around the tablecloth.

NEIGHBOUR 1: Here's to the soldiers!

ALL: To the soldiers!

They all mime drinking a toast. They sip their soup, small sips at first. They nod at each other and then start drinking the soup faster and faster, with appropriate sounds. The SOLDIERS drink soup too. They finish together with a big sigh.

VILLAGER 1: That...

VILLAGER 2: ... was...

VILLAGER 3: ... the...

VILLAGER 4: ... most...

VILLAGER 5: ... delicious ...

VILLAGER 6: ... soup...

ALL: ... we have ever tasted!

Sources

The Tug of War
Based on a traditional story of the trickster Hare found in many versions across South and East Africa, including one told by Michael Rosen in *South and North, East and West* (Walker Books, London, 1992).

The Strongest Person in the World
An adaptation of the traditional story *The White Rat* found in variations across Asia and Europe, retold by Michael Rosen in *South and North, East and West* (Walker Books, London, 1992).

The Midas Touch
Based on the Greek myth by the poet Ovid, dating back to the 8th century.

Why the Hippopotamus Wears No Coat
Based on a traditional story from the Krobo people of Ghana found in *West African Folktales* by Jack Berry (Northwestern University Press, Evanston, Illinois, 1991).

The Hungry Coat and The Talking Donkey
These two plays are based on the popular stories of Nasreddin Hodja, a philosopher and wise man said to come from Aksehir, Turkey – although many countries across Asia claim him as their own.

The Musicians of Bremen
Based on a folktale recorded by the Brothers Grimm.

Stone Soup
Based on a traditional story found in many variations across Europe and Scandinavia.

Glossary

Auditorium The area where the audience sits to watch the play.

Blocking The mapping of movement by the actors around the stage.

Business Any action(s) carried out by an actor during the performance, such as knocking on a door.

Cast All the performers in a play.

Choreographer The person who directs movement and dance by the performers.

Cross To move from one side of the stage to the other.

Cue An action carried out or a line spoken by an actor immediately before another character speaks.

Designer The person responsible for designing the set, costumes and props.

Director The person who instructs and advises the actors during rehearsals.

Ensemble A type of performance where all members of the cast work together to create scenes, images and effects.

Focus The point on the stage that the director wants the audience to look at.

FX Abbreviation for "effects" including sound, special (SFX) and lighting (LX).

Green Room A room for the actors to relax in when they are not on stage.

Line Run A run through of the play without any action so that the actors can practise their lines.

Musical Director The person who chooses and rehearses the music and songs in a play.

Pace The speed of the actors' actions and words.

Projection (voice) The ability to speak loudly and clearly to all members of the audience.

Prop A small or large object used in a play.

Set The scenery and furniture used in a play.

Sight Lines The action visible to all members of the audience, including those sitting at the edges of the auditorium.

Sound Cue The sound effect or music played just before a particular moment in a play.

Speed Run A rehearsal of the play by the actors at high speed (words and movement) in order to practice the cues and blocking.

Stage Directions The words in the script which describe what the actors should do or how they should act.

Stage Manager The person responsible for organising all the props and costumes.

Stage Picture The overall image created by the actors and director at a particular moment.

Understudy Someone who learns the part of another actor in case they are unable to perform.

About the Author

Based in Norwich, Norfolk, David Farmer trained as a primary school teacher then worked in theatre-in-education as an actor, writer and director. In 1981 he co-founded *Tiebreak Theatre Company* and was Artistic Director until 2005, producing over 65 acclaimed plays and projects that reached an audience of half a million young people in schools, theatres and festivals. These included commissions by the *Lyric Theatre Hammersmith* and the *Natural History Museum*, sell-out performances at the *Edinburgh Fringe Festival* and tours across Europe, Canada and the USA.

David is a freelance drama consultant, delivering training to teachers, actors, directors and students in the UK and abroad. He has mentored projects for *Drama for Learning and Creativity*, *Shakespeare Schools Festival* and *Creative Partnerships*. He leads drama projects with school children, directs community plays and is a regular contributor to magazines such as *Teaching Drama*. His first three books are now a part of the national curriculum in Trinidad and Tobago.

Drama Resource

The author's website at **www.DramaResource.com** contains ever-growing resources for teaching drama – including games, strategies, lesson plans and one-day courses where you are invited to experience and explore these ideas with like-minded people. You can also sign up to the free *Drama Resource Newsletter* bringing monthly news and resources to your desktop.

Lightning Source UK Ltd.
Milton Keynes UK
UKHW02f1841210318

319851UK00027B/1482/P